D0031216

TOO YOUNG TO ESCAPE

Too young to Escape

A Vietnamese Girl Waits to be Reunited with Her Family

Van Ho and
Marsha Forchuk Skrypuch

pajamapress

First published in Canada and the United States in 2018

www.pajamapress.ca   info@pajamapress.ca

 Canada Council   Conseil des arts
for the Arts   du Canada    ONTARIO ARTS COUNCIL
CONSEIL DES ARTS DE L'ONTARIO
an Ontario government agency
un organisme du gouvernement de l'Ontario    Canadä

The publisher gratefully acknowledges the support of the Canada Council for the Arts and the Ontario Arts Council for its publishing program. We acknowledge the financial support of the Government of Canada through the Canada Book Fund (CBF) for our publishing activities.

Library and Archives Canada Cataloguing in Publication

Ho, Van, 1977-, author
    Too young to escape : a Vietnamese girl waits to be reunited with her family / Van Ho and Marsha Forchuk Skrypuch. -- First edition.

ISBN 978-1-77278-066-6 (hardcover)

    1. Ho, Van, 1977- --Childhood and youth--Juvenile literature. 2. Vietnam War, 1961-1975--Children--Juvenile literature. 3. Vietnam War, 1961-1975-- Biography--Juvenile literature. 4. Refugee children--Vietnam--Juvenile literature. I. Skrypuch, Marsha Forchuk, 1954-, author II. Title.

DS559.914.H62T66 2018   j959.704'4092   C2018-902709-6

Publisher Cataloging-in-Publication Data (U.S.)

Names: Ho, Van, 1977-, author. | Forchuk Skrypuch, Marsha, author.
Title: Too Young to Escape : A Vietnamese Girl Waits to be Reunited with Her Family / Van Ho and Marsha Forchuk Skrypuch.
Description: Toronto, Ontario Canada : Pajama Press, 2018. | Summary: "After the Vietnam War, a young girl is left behind in the care of her grandmother when the rest of her family flees the new communist regime by boat. Once settled in North America, her parents will send for her; but in the meantime, Van must work for her demanding aunt and uncle, who treat her like a servant. And she is forced to deal with the school bully, who is the son of a military policeman"— Provided by publisher.
Identifiers: ISBN 978-1-77278-066-6 (hardcover)
Subjects: LCSH: Ho, Van – Juvenile literature. | Vietnam War, 1961-1975— Refugees – Juvenile literature. | Bullying – Juvenile literature. | BISAC: JUVENILE NONFICTION / Biography & Autobiography / Cultural Heritage. | JUVENILE NONFICTION / Social Topics / Emigration & Immigration.
Classification: LCC DS559.914.H |DDC 959.7044092 – dc23

Cover and interior illustrations: Brian Deines
Photos: courtesy of Vanessa Ho
Cover and book design: Rebecca Buchanan, and Martin Gould / martingould.com

Manufactured by Friesens
Printed in Canada

Pajama Press Inc.
181 Carlaw Ave., Suite 251, Toronto, Ontario Canada, M4M 2S1

Distributed in Canada by UTP Distribution
5201 Dufferin Street Toronto, Ontario Canada, M3H 5T8

Distributed in the U.S. by Ingram Publisher Services
1 Ingram Blvd. La Vergne, TN 37086, USA

33614080896243

DEDICATIONS

IN LOVING MEMORY of Bà Ngoại, who was a rock throughout my life. You took care of me, and supported me through good times and bad. I am the person I am today largely because of you. Thank you for your unconditional love, thank you for your support, thank you for being my Bà Ngoại. I love you more than words can say.

–V. H.

FOR THOSE whose voices are a whisper.

–M. F. S.

CHAPTER ONE
Like Any Other Day

MAY 19, 1981, HO CHI MINH CITY

It was five o'clock. The rooster crowed, waking me up as usual. Ma and my older sisters were already gone. They often woke up early and went off to do their work. Auntie Phuong and her daughters shared the third floor sleeping area of the house with all of us. But as they usually kept the same hours as Ma, it didn't seem unusual that they were also gone.

But Tuan wasn't here.

My six-year-old brother almost never got up so early. Still, I didn't think much of it. Every now and then he had something special to do with his friends.

So that morning, only my grandmother, Bà Ngoại, and I still lay on our bamboo mats.

Bà Ngoại must have heard the rooster too. I closed my eyes and listened to her go through her usual routine. She filled the pot with water for me and put it on the charcoal burner to warm. She didn't wait for warm water for herself. Instead, she quickly washed with cold water in the shower stall at the end of our room. Then she dressed and crept down the two flights of stairs to go to the market.

I got up and swallowed down a dose of the bitter liquid that loosened the phlegm in my lungs. I took a lot of different medicines to help me with breathing, but this tarry syrup was the worst. After I swallowed, I coughed and coughed, spitting up phlegm into the sink. I tried to cough quietly so I wouldn't wake my aunt and uncle, who slept below us on the second floor. Dì and Bác owned the house and Ma often reminded me that we were their guests.

I took off my shorts and shirt from yesterday, then filled a pail with the warm water to take into the shower. Using the bath cup, I rinsed off the sheen of sticky sweat that had accumulated over the hot night. I made a lather with the bar of soap, and scrubbed my face, neck, and body. I left my hair alone—I only washed it on Sunday. I rinsed off, using one cup of warm water at a time, watching it swirl down the drain. I dried myself with the towel that was still damp from Bà Ngoại's bath. Then I slipped into a fresh set of clothes. Even when yesterday's clothes seemed fresh enough for me, Ma insisted that we change. "We may be poor," she said. "But we will always be clean and fresh."

I crept down to the second-floor landing. Bác's slippers were lined up neatly just outside his bedroom door. I picked up the slippers and stepped in through the door without making a sound. I tiptoed over to my uncle's mat. One of his arms was flung loosely across my aunt's shoulder. Both of their faces were slack with sleep. Neither of them roused as I silently put his slippers down on his side of the mat. I stepped out again, holding my breath until I was back in the hallway. I paused for a moment and listened through the door. Nothing but rhythmic breathing and light snores.

I exhaled in relief. I had completed my first chore of the morning.

Girl guests were expected to do many chores, even four-year-old girl guests.

I had to pee, but I was afraid to go to the outhouse in the dark. At least down on the main floor it was cooler than in our cramped sleeping area. I sat down at my spindle and carefully twisted a new tuft of coarse black fiber and attached it to the length of yesterday's finished yarn that hung from the spinning wheel. With great care, I cranked the wheel and guided the tufts of fiber through the hole, so it would be twisted and turned into yarn.

Since the war ended and the communists took over all the businesses, the only way Dì and Bác could make ends meet was by bartering things on the street and making and selling rice sacks from their house. The war ended before I was born, but Ma said that she and Ba and all the aunts and uncles had lost everything. Dì and Bác still had this house, and they let us all live there with them.

The rice sacks were woven and sewn in the middle room on the main floor of the house. I had to spin enough yarn every morning before school so that when the weaver came, she'd have lots of yarn to make cloth. She worked on a loom that took up about a third of the work area. Then another worker would cut the fabric and sew it into bags. The finished bags were stacked against the wall until the customer wanted them. At times that stack would be taller than me.

When I first began to do the spinning months ago, my fingers were so tender that they would get tiny cuts on the tips from the rough fiber. The blood didn't show on the black yarn, but Dì was furious when she saw it. Now my fingertips were callused enough that they no longer bled, but sometimes Dì would still look at my work and frown. "It's too loose here," she'd say angrily, and I would cringe. I learned to spin perfectly. I didn't want to get Dì and Bác angry.

By the time Bà Ngoại came back from the market with her wicker bag full of greens for breakfast, my ball of yarn was the size of a fist. I kept spinning as she coaxed a fire from the charcoal embers in the main kitchen behind my work area. She put on a big pot of rice to cook. I spun my yarn as, humming under her breath, she chopped bamboo shoots, garlic, and broccoli. The scent of fresh garlic and rice filled the air. My stomach grumbled. But I was also keenly aware of how badly I needed to go to the outhouse. It was still dark outside, though, so I kept on holding it in and continued spinning fiber into yarn.

The sun lightened the room around six o'clock, but I kept spinning for another couple of hours until my ball of yarn was as wide as a rice hat.

What was I thinking that day?

When I heard Dì and Bác on the second floor make waking noises, I got up from the floor and stretched the stiffness out of my legs. I had to use the outhouse before they came downstairs. I knew that it was better to stay out of their way.

I stepped through the curtain to the kitchen and was enveloped in the steamy scent of garlic. "Good morning, Bà Ngoại," I said to my grandmother as I hurried past her.

My bladder felt like it was about to burst, but I hated going to the outhouse, especially in the dark. Huge spiders collected on the ceiling. The thought of one dropping down on me in the dark was terrifying. Now that it was light outside, at least I could see them.

I squatted over the dirt hole and looked up. I counted the spiders—five today. I kept my eyes on them as I finished. None of them dropped down on me. I ran out, glad to get that over with for another morning.

I washed my hands in the kitchen sink, and Bà Ngoại set out a bowl of rice and vegetables for me. I ate half, then wrapped what was left in a dishtowel and took it, along with my chopsticks, upstairs. It felt good to have a full stomach and the spinning done.

I put the chopsticks and leftover rice and vegetables in my backpack. I wet my index finger, dipped it in a small bowl of salt, and used it to brush my teeth.

I ran down the stairs, eager to leave for school. But I wasn't finished quite yet. My spinning earlier had created little bits of fiber that floated in the air and covered the floor and furniture. Dust from outside also came in past the metal grilles on the windows. Dì would not be happy if she saw my dust. With a damp cloth, I wiped down each fancy enamel chair and the inlaid coffee table. I also dusted the window grilles. I wondered where my sisters Loan and Lan were. They usually swept the floor and dusted the walls. I didn't have time to do that by myself before school. I could only hope that Dì and Bác wouldn't be upset when they realized the work hadn't been finished.

CHAPTER TWO
Where Are They?

WITH MY MORNING CHORES finally complete, I pushed open the front door and burst onto the Nguyễn Trãi Street of Ho Chi Minh City. Immediately I was surrounded by a cacophony of horns and shouts. The gutters swirled with garbage, giving off a smell of putrid fat and rotting fish. A crush of people walked shoulder to shoulder. They smelled of old sweat, garlic, and stale tobacco. I kept close to the houses and away from the bicyclists, who wove their way precariously around pedestrians and scooters. Some of the cyclists balanced large boxes that sat on their handlebars or were strapped behind their seats. I also watched out for cyclos—three-wheeled bicycles with a two-person passenger seat in front of the handlebars. Like the bicyclists, the cyclo drivers carried many things besides people: a goat, a pig, building supplies, or farm produce. Bicyclists and cyclo drivers had one thing in common—they were always in a hurry.

Usually, Tuan would walk to school with me. I hated to go by myself.

School was three blocks away. The building was a wide one-storey that looked not all that different from the houses and stores close by. To the side was a large paved area where students could play until it was time to go in.

When I reached the schoolyard, I leaned against the wall and tried to look as if I was intensely interested in watching the clouds in the sky. Summer break would start at the end of May and I was counting down the days.

Two girls from my class turned a rope and a third girl jumped in, skipping in rhythm. Once, she missed her step and they had to start over. But instead of getting upset with herself, she just laughed. How I would have loved to be that brave. I wished I could run over there and join them, but I was much too shy. Those three girls seemed like such good friends. They didn't even notice me. In some ways, maybe it was best that they didn't notice me. What if I did skip with them and had a coughing fit? It would be too embarrassing to vomit phlegm at school.

The bell rang, and the kids formed neat lines, entering the building as each class was called. While I waited, I searched the faces of the kids lined up beside me, looking for Tuan. He wasn't there.

When Loan's class was called in, I stood on my tiptoes and watched as each of her classmates entered the school. Her best friend Sen waved at me, but my sister wasn't there.

And then Lan's class was called in. She was missing too.

Of all my family, I was the only one at school that day. If it had just been my sisters, it wouldn't have been that unusual. Girls had other work to do, after all. But my brother? According to Ma, his most important job was to get an education.

Where could they all be? And why wasn't I included?

I kept in step with the rest of my class when it was our turn to march single file through the doors and down the hallway. Our classroom was just a few yards from the entrance. Mrs. Nguyen insisted that our desks be lined up perfectly. I walked in and sat down at my desk, which was in the middle of the second row.

As I waited for everyone to settle in, I stared up at the portrait on the wall of Ho Chi Minh. At school, the adults told us that he was our great leader. But at home, nobody said anything nice about him. I knew from whispers between Ma and Bà Ngoại that Ho Chi Minh was the reason we had lost our home and why we were now forced to live as guests with Dì and Bác. But when I looked up at his picture in my class, I thought his eyes seemed kind.

I knew Ho Chi Minh's face better than my own father's. Ba had left us a year ago, taking my oldest sister Linh with him. Sometimes at night I would dream of Ba, but his face was just a blur. All I remembered for certain was that Ba smelled of charcoal and was much kinder than Bác. Ma told me that Ba had translated Vietnamese into English for the Americans during the war, and the communists wanted to kill him for that. So he had to escape.

Mrs. Nguyen clapped her hands. "Stand, young comrades."

We scrambled out of our desks and stood at attention. Together, we pledged to uphold Ho Chi Minh's five teachings: to love the fatherland, study well, obey the teacher, stay clean, and be truthful.

After that, I took out my chalk slate and practiced writing my letters as Mrs. Nguyen called them out: a ă â b e ê g...

Numbers came after, then singing. It was like any other day. Mostly, I looked out the window and watched the clouds change shape. And I prayed that Mrs. Nguyen wouldn't ask me a question or rap my knuckles with her ruler for not paying attention.

And I wondered where my family had gone.

When the bell rang for lunch, I took my bowl and chopsticks outside and found a shady place to sit by myself. I leaned against the wall and enjoyed the fresh air. I scooped up a lump of rice with my chopsticks and popped it into my mouth, chewing slowly, savoring the taste.

When school ended, I slung my knapsack over my shoulder and walked all by myself back through the busy streets, making sure to stay close to the buildings and away from the traffic.

I stepped in through the kitchen at Dì and Bác's house and closed the door behind me. It was like stepping into another time. The noisy street sounds were muffled by the sizzle of Bà Ngoại's wok. My stomach grumbled and I breathed in deeply, appreciating the rich aroma of fried meat with spices. This was the scent of home.

Bà Ngoại looked up, her knife poised above a head of bok choy. Her face was covered in a sheen of sweat, and her gray hair was tightly braided into a bun on the top of her head. Sometimes it seemed as if Bà Ngoại's entire day was filled with shopping for food or preparing food.

She set her knife down and smiled. "I'm glad to have you home, little one."

I put my backpack on the floor and took out my lunch bowl and chopsticks. As I washed them in the sink beside her, I asked, "Is Ma home yet?"

"No," said Bà Ngoại. She sighed and turned to face me. Her smile had disappeared. "She's gone to Canada, to be with your Ba and Linh."

Her words made no sense. Ba and Linh had disappeared long ago. They no longer seemed real to me. But Ma *was* real. She comforted me when I was sad. She was always there for me.

I was almost too shocked to speak.

"Will she sleep with me tonight?" I whispered.

A crinkle formed on Bà Ngoại's brow. "She's not coming back, little one."

I held my hand up to my face and pinched it, grimacing at the sharp pain. My hand was real. Ma was real. Ma was *part* of me, just like my hand. But I knew better than to argue with an adult.

"What about Tuan and my sisters?" I said slowly. "Do you think that they have gone to Canada too?"

Bà Ngoại nodded. She didn't seem upset or surprised.

Right then, I longed to yell and scream and cry. But I took a deep breath to calm myself. I could not show what I felt. Instead, I stomped up the stairs to begin my afternoon chores.

I refused to believe her.

CHAPTER THREE
Afternoon Chores

THERE WASN'T TIME in the morning before school to clean Dì and Bác's bedroom, so I had to do the work now, before they got home.

My aunt and uncle's room was spacious and airy. It was much cooler than our own sleeping space on the floor above. I pushed the bed to make it line up straight with the wall, then rolled up the bamboo mat so I could dust the wooden base. Then I shook the bamboo mat over the side of the balcony wall to make sure it was clean. Since I was so short, the only way to do that was to stand on my toes and hold the mat with a tight grip so I wouldn't lose it. Once it was shaken out, I rolled the mat back up and carried it to the bed. I unrolled it onto the wooden frame, then shook out the blankets, pillowcases, and pillows over the side of the balcony. I hated touching all their bedding because spiders liked to hide in folds of cloth. But I was more afraid of Dì and Bác's anger than spiders. My aunt and uncle would be mad if one of them was bitten because I didn't do my job. After airing the linens and making the bed, I dusted the walls and tables, and swept the floor.

Next, I took a damp cloth and got on my hands and knees and carefully cleaned the nooks and corners where the floor met the walls, making sure not to leave a single speck of dust.

Usually Ma or my sisters would have stepped in to help me when they got home. But Ma never appeared, and neither did Lan or Loan. It took me much longer than usual to do all the work.

Was Bà Ngoại right? Had my family really left me behind?

When I was finished cleaning Dì and Bác's bedroom, I hurried downstairs to clean the front room. I needed to finish it before my aunt and uncle got home.

But Dì was standing in the living room, hands on hips, her forehead creased in anger.

"I give you a roof over your head and food to eat," she said. "All I ask in exchange is that you help around the house. Why haven't you dusted this room yet?"

"I was just about to start," I said, holding up my dusting cloth as proof.

She slapped me, hard, on the side of my face.

"You are a bad girl."

The shock of the slap made me almost lose my balance. I steadied myself and kept my gaze to the floor. I felt like crying, like running away, but that would only make it worse.

"I'm sorry," I said.

"Obedience is all I ask," said Dì. Then she turned and left the room.

My cheek stung, but I took a deep breath and ignored the pain. I had to get on with my work. Dust had settled all over the living room since the morning, so I carefully wiped down each fancy enamel chair in the front room with a damp cloth. Then I polished the inlaid coffee table with lemon oil. I dusted the window grilles and walls, and swept the floor. The room was perfect by the time I finished.

I paused at the kitchen curtain and listened. Was Dì in there with Bà Ngoại? I heard only my grandmother humming under her breath as she chopped up vegetables. I stepped in. Without a word to Bà Ngoại, I grabbed the broom and began to sweep the floor, making sure to get into the corners so that Dì and Bác would have nothing to complain about.

The chopping stopped and Bà Ngoại rested her hand on my shoulder. "Was it Dì who slapped you?" she whispered.

I nodded.

"You and I both will have more work to do, now that your ma and sisters are gone," she said in a loud voice, as if she knew Dì might be listening from another room. "Let's do the best we can."

I nodded again, my eyes filling with tears.

"Enough," said Bà Ngoại gently, drying my face with the corner of her dishcloth.

I finished sweeping the kitchen floor in silence, then wiped down the counter. By the time I finished, my lungs were full of phlegm. Gasping for breath, I pulled myself up the three flights of stairs. When I stepped into our own room, everything was changed. The seven bamboo beds that had covered the entire floor area of our cramped room had been taken apart and were now stacked in the corner. Bà Ngoại had probably tidied up while I was at school. Just two beds now sat side by side, made up neatly. I lay on my bed, feeling as empty as the room looked. My cheek throbbed.

Why would Ma disappear without even saying good-bye? And why did she leave *me*? Maybe I had been a bad girl, and this was my punishment. But what had I done? I hadn't *meant* to be bad.

I clutched my pillow and wept. I felt as if my heart were broken in two.

CHAPTER FOUR
Left Behind

I DON'T REMEMBER much about supper that night. I sat at the big table downstairs with Dì and Bác, while Bà Ngoại placed food in front of us. I must have eaten some of it, but I really don't remember. What I do remember is Dì saying that my family was on a dangerous journey.

"Please, Daughter," Bà Ngoại said to Dì. "Let us not talk about that in front of Van."

Dì picked up a morsel of fish with her chopsticks and chewed on it slowly, her gaze falling on me. "It will be less crowded here," she said. "And cooler in your bedroom without so many people."

Bà Ngoại nodded. "That is true, Daughter."

"It will be cheaper for food too," Dì said. "But there are still the same number of chores." She pointed her chopstick at me. "You need to be a good girl and keep up."

Her words made me cringe. I kept my eyes on my rice bowl and said, "Yes, Aunt. I will do better."

Why had Ma left me here but taken my brother and sisters? Dì said I was a bad girl. Maybe Ma thought I was a bad girl too. Maybe she left me because she was angry with me. When the meal was finished, I lingered in the kitchen, helping Bà Ngoại to wash the dishes. I was desperate to find out more about Ma.

Once the kitchen was clean, I followed on Bà Ngoại's heels up to the third floor, where the sight of those seven beds stacked in the corner made the sorrow crash into me again. I waited for Bà Ngoại to settle on her mat, then snuggled in beside her. We lay together, wrapped in the lingering scent of garlic and lemongrass. I was comforted by the familiar sinewy strength of Bà Ngoại's arms wrapped around my waist.

"You are loved, my granddaughter," she said, kissing the top of my head. "Don't ever forget that."

"Did Ma go away because I was bad?"

"No," said Bà Ngoại.

"Then why did they leave me?"

"Dì told the truth," said Bà Ngoại. "Escaping by boat is dangerous, especially for young children."

"Why did they go if it's so dangerous?" I asked.

"Because it's dangerous here too."

I had been born after the war, but Ma had told me what it had been like before. Ba and Ma had a business and a house and enough food. They lost everything when South Vietnam lost the war. That's why we lived as guests with Dì and Bác.

"But if it's dangerous to stay, why did they leave *me*? Is it dangerous for me here?"

"We will just have to be careful not to attract the attention of the military police. Your turn to leave will come, little one, when you're older." She rested her chin on my head. "Sometimes there are no perfect solutions. Once your mother is safe in Canada, she and your father will arrange for you to join them."

I didn't understand what Bà Ngoại meant by that. All I knew was that Ma had disappeared. I got up from

Bà Ngoại's mat and climbed into my own bed, clutching my pillow close, pretending I was hugging Ma.

I did eventually fall asleep. But a vivid dream came to me: I stood in the middle of a busy street with speeding bicycles and cars all around. I tried to run, but my feet had roots like trees and I couldn't move. "Ma, Ma, help me," I cried.

But Ma didn't come.

CHAPTER FIVE
Without Them

THE REST OF MAY disappeared in a lonely haze of spinning, school, chores, and homework. At night I would hug my pillow and cry for Ma. My sadness covered me like a shroud. I wondered if others could even see that I existed. The only way I knew I was still alive was when I looked in Bà Ngoại's eyes and saw her love shine back at me. She was my anchor. My rock.

When school ended on the last day of May, I suddenly had chunks of empty time. When school had occupied my days, it was Ma that I missed most. But now that school was over, my heart ached at the memory of the previous summer, and all the things I did with Tuan and Lan and Loan.

I had spent hours shooting elastics across the floor with Tuan to see whose would go the farthest. Tuan usually won, but only because he was older. I didn't mind. Sometimes we'd go to the market and watch other kids buy sweets. We imagined what it must be like to have enough money to waste on things like that. Other times, we'd go the schoolyard and I'd watch Tuan kick a ball with his friends. If none of his friends showed up, he'd kick the ball with me. That was a special day.

Money had been tight for as long as I could remember, so we each got only one piece of meat a day. Tuan was always hungry, and he would gobble his right up. Then he would distract me and steal my piece of meat. I used to get so angry with him! Now, I'd give him all my meat if only he would come back. I even missed the days when Tuan was mean to me.

I remembered times with my sisters too, chatting and laughing while I helped Lan with the mending or Loan with the washing. With Loan and Lan gone, the mending and washing were just more lonely chores.

The emptiness of my days yawned in front of me. I still missed Ma most of all, but I also wanted Tuan and Loan and Lan to come back.

I tagged behind Bà Ngoại in the kitchen as she cooked and cleaned, trying to help her. I was afraid to be alone with my sad thoughts.

Sometimes, she let me come with her to the market, and I loved that. She would carry her wicker basket, and I would take a net bag.

I loved walking through the food vendors' section of the market. My stomach growled when I inhaled the steamy smoke of the many different delicious seasonings and sizzling meats and seafood. The market was crammed with vendors selling every imaginable kind of food. Pork patties sizzled on charcoal grills, and steaming vats of *phở* were ladled out to customers one soup bowl at a time. Once, Bà Ngoại treated me to *bạch tuộc nướng*—a delicious spicy grilled octopus. But usually we would have a bowl of either *phở,* or *bánh canh cua*—a hearty fish stew. Another favorite was *bánh xèo*, a crispy fried pancake. Together, we would eat and listen to the babble of customers.

Around the corner from the food vendors was the

part of the market where fresh fish and meat were sold. I always held my breath as long as I could. But no matter how hard I tried not to inhale, I still ended up gasping in at least one giant gulp of rotten fish smell.

The next part of the market was for fruit and vegetable vendors. Here, almost everything smelled good. Bà Ngoại would pick through the cabbage, garlic, bitter melon, and spinach, and load up my net bag. She would select fruits too, and there were lots to choose from: pineapple and dragon fruit, mangoes and star apples, papaya and coconut. Everything smelled good, except for one fruit called durian, or corpse fruit. It smelled like poop, but tasted sweet and creamy.

In the summer, there was more time to go to temple as well. Bà Ngoại liked the Giác Lâm Pagoda the best, but it was quite a distance from our house. She would hail a three-wheeled cyclo and I'd grip the sides of our seat as our cyclist wove in and out through the narrow gaps between speeding vehicles, stalled cars, and goats tethered with rope.

Once we arrived outside the temple, Bà Ngoại would light three sticks of incense, called joss sticks, for herself and three for me, handling them carefully so they would smoke but not burn. I would take my three sticks in the palms of my hands and hold them to my forehead. As I faced the temple doors, I would bow and pray for Ma to come home. Bà Ngoại would say her prayers as well. When we were finished, we would throw the smoking joss sticks into a huge metal basin in the courtyard.

We would then step through the temple doors, which were painted with giant dragons. Once inside, Bà Ngoại would choose four candles from the rack against the wall. She'd light two and give them to me, then she would light two for herself. We would bow and pray once again, before blowing out the candles and putting them back on the rack. I would follow Bà Ngoại as she went from one pillar to the next, paying tribute at the altars of holy people and reading the engraved gold script that told the ancient history of our people. I loved visiting the statues of all the different Buddhas, and reading each of their stories.

It brought me comfort to visit the temple. My own problems would suddenly appear smaller.

CHAPTER SIX
A Friend

WHEN SCHOOL STARTED again in September, my classmates seemed to be mostly the same from the year before. But as each of us stood up in class to introduce ourselves, I saw that we had one new girl. Her name was Trang. Her clothing was more worn and faded than most of the others'. I was suddenly conscious of my own clothes and how they must look. Usually Ma would have bought me one new outfit to start school. But Bà Ngoại had little money, so I was forced to make do with my old hand-me-downs.

Our new teacher, Mrs. Le, was taller than Mrs. Nguyen. She had black-framed glasses and wore her gray hair pulled into a bun. She liked to whack her ruler on the edge of her desk to get our attention.

At recess on the first day back, Chie'n, who had been a classmate of Tuan's, walked past me with something cupped in his hands. A cluster of boys followed close on his heels. He knelt on the pavement a yard or so in front of me and opened his hands. A cricket hopped out.

"Anyone else find one?" he asked, smiling up at his friends.

Another boy pushed through the group and knelt beside him. "I've got a cricket. Let's race them."

"Whichever cricket goes from here to here wins," said Chie'n, placing two rulers about a foot apart from each other.

The other boy placed his cricket next to Chie'n's, and their friends crouched on their hands and knees, jostling for the front row. I could see over the boys' shoulders, so both crickets were in clear view.

"I bet Chie'n's is going to win," shouted one boy.

Another said, "My bet's on Gia's cricket."

But the crickets just sat there.

Chie'n took out a pencil and poked his cricket,

but it still wouldn't move. He poked it again. It hopped.

Half of the boys cheered.

Gia's cricket hopped once, and then again. The other boys cheered.

I thought it was a silly thing to get all excited about, but I wasn't a boy.

Just then, Trang hesitated at the outer edge of the cluster. The new girl held her lunch of rice wrapped in a palm leaf with both hands, and she leaned over to see the cricket race.

Chie'n poked his cricket with the pencil a third time, but the insect didn't budge. Gia's cricket took off, hopping madly all the way to the other ruler. Cheers and shouts erupted.

"No fair," said Chie'n, flashing an angry look at Gia. "Your cricket is younger than mine."

"Don't be such a poor sport," said Gia. "My cricket won fair and square."

Chie'n's face and neck flushed with anger. He banged his fist down on Gia's cricket and crushed it.

Suddenly everyone went silent. It was as if they all held their breath at the same time. No one wanted to get on Chie'n's bad side. Even Gia said nothing, even though it was his cricket that Chie'n crushed.

"That wasn't very nice," blurted Trang.

One boy gasped.

Chie'n stood up and stepped in front of Trang. "You're just a girl. Shut up!" And he punched her in the shoulder with his cricket-smeared fist.

Trang fell hard onto the pavement. Her lunch flew out of her hand and landed in front of me.

Chie'n grinned. "That will teach you."

The cluster of boys was quiet for a moment. But then a couple of them began to laugh before they all scattered.

I picked up Trang's palm leaf of rice and dusted it off. "What a bully he is," I said, helping her up. "I wonder why those other boys seem to like him so much."

Trang got up awkwardly and dusted the dirt off the back of her shorts and the smear of dead cricket from her shirt.

"Maybe they're afraid of him," she said, following me back to the shady spot against the wall.

We ate our lunch in silence. I felt sorry for Trang. I

wished I had been brave enough to say something to Chie'n instead of just watching him punch her.

Trang turned to me. "Thanks," she said. "It's good of you to let me sit with you."

"I like sitting with you too," I told her. It was nice to have lunch with someone instead of all by myself.

When we walked back to our class in the afternoon, Trang took her seat—along the same row as mine but at the very back. *Maybe Trang will be my friend,* I thought.

The afternoon's lessons ticked by slowly. I stared out the window and watched the fluffy clouds as they shifted and floated and took on many different shapes. I recited back what Mrs. Le instructed us to repeat, and I copied down onto my slate the numbers and letters we needed to practice. When the bell finally rang, I exited the school with my classmates. Instead of rushing home as usual, I walked slowly through the schoolyard toward the exit on Le Trang Rieng Street.

"Which way do you go home?" asked Trang, catching up from behind.

"I'm on the other side of the block, on Nguyen Trai Street," I told her. Our house was almost directly behind the school, but I had to walk three blocks to get to it. "Which way do you live?"

"That way," Trang said, pointing east. "We live on Bui Trang Xuan Street just where it merges with Le Trang Rieng Street."

"What time do you get here in the morning?" I asked.

"About fifteen minutes before the bell rings," she said.

"Maybe I'll see you tomorrow before class, then," I said.

She smiled broadly. "That would be great."

All the way home, I couldn't help smiling. I still missed Ma and my sisters and brother. But having a friend would be nice.

CHAPTER SEVEN
Wearing Rags

WEEKS TURNED to months with no word from Ma. I tried not to think about her because it only made me sad. But the new school year was a little bit better than I thought it would be, mostly because I had one friend. I was still sad and lonely at home, but at least during recess and lunchtime, I could play with Trang.

Bà Ngoại had some money saved up, and I think Ma gave her everything she could before she left. But my medicine was expensive and so were my schoolbooks. I knew that Bà Ngoại hoped my parents would be able to send money soon. We didn't expect Dì and Bác to help out with my expenses.

One morning, as I stepped into a fresh pair of shorts for school, my thumb went right through some of the fabric around the waistband. I took the shorts off, folded them, and placed them in the mending basket. I would have to remember to fix them when I got back home. I took out my last pair of clean shorts. As I pulled them on, I could see just how fragile the fabric in all my clothing had become. All three t-shirts and pairs of shorts had faded and worn thin with time and washing. I had grown quite a bit since they had been passed down to me from Lan. Now all my clothes were tight, and that put a strain on the fabric as well.

I pulled a clean t-shirt over my head, careful not to tug at it too much, then started on my morning chores.

At the schoolyard, I stood there for a moment and watched the kids running around and playing. Even though most of the students were dressed in simple t-shirts, shorts, and flip-flops—like me—it seemed as if no one looked as shabby as me.

Just then, Trang ran up and grabbed my hand. "Three of the older girls have an elastic jump rope," she said. "Let's go watch."

As we walked through the schoolyard together, I looked at Trang out of the corner of my eye and realized that my clothes were every bit as shabby as hers. It made me feel bad for both of us, but deep down it also made me feel just a little bit better knowing I wasn't the only one wearing rags to school.

One humid day a few weeks later, the air was so thick that it made me gasp. I leaned against the wall and tried to catch my breath while Trang told me about a big accident she'd seen on the way to school that morning. I was almost glad when the bell rang and it was time go back inside. At least then I'd be able to sit down.

As we were lining up, Chie'n elbowed past me. In the crush of students, his hand caught on my shorts and I felt a rip.

"Oops," said Chie'n, grinning. Then he scrambled away to stand innocently in his own class lineup.

Trang stepped in behind me. "Just walk," she said quietly. "I'll keep close behind you and no one will see."

"Is my underwear showing?" I whispered.

"Just a little bit," she said. "Your shorts are ripped up the seam."

The two of us shuffled forward, and I somehow got into my seat without drawing attention to myself. Thank goodness that Trang had been there to help me.

Mrs. Le walked into the room and faced the class. "Young comrades, take out your songbooks and stand," she said. "Turn to page nine. We will sing, 'Proceed Under The Flag.'"

My heart sank. I had hoped to get through the afternoon without having to stand up. I grabbed my songbook and put it on top of my desk. Then, with one hand, I tried to hold the back of my shorts together as I stood up.

Someone giggled behind me.

Mrs. Le slammed her ruler down, making a loud *thwacking* noise. "No laughing," she said.

The giggling stopped, but I could feel all eyes on my bum. We practiced the song over and over until Mrs. Le felt that we knew it thoroughly. "Sit, young comrades," she said. "And take out your chalk slates."

I sank down thankfully into my chair. When it was

finally time to go home, I waited until everyone but Trang had left.

"Stand up," Trang said. "Let's figure out how you can strap your knapsack so it hangs low enough to hide the rip."

It took some arranging, but we managed to sling the knapsack low enough to cover my bum. We exited the school together and walked to the end of the yard. As she turned toward her street, I waved good-bye, then went on alone. I had barely gone half a block when Chie'n stepped out from an alleyway.

"That's a funny way to wear a knapsack." He tugged on one of the straps and it slipped off my shoulder. I pushed it back up, then stepped to the left to walk around Chie'n. But he darted in front of me, blocking my way. I stepped to the right; so did he.

"Stop that!" I shouted. The words startled me as much as they startled him. No one talked to Chie'n that way at school. I clutched both straps of my knapsack and plunged ahead. My shoulder bumped into him, but I kept on going.

I only managed to walk quickly for half a block before I started to cough. Soon I was doubled over. As

I tried to catch my breath, I turned to look for Chie'n.

But he had disappeared.

When I finally got home and into the kitchen, I burst into tears as soon as I saw my grandmother. She set down her knife and gathered me into her arms. "What's the matter, little one?" she asked.

"I need a new pair of shorts," I said, turning around and showing her my bum.

"I've been trying to save money," said Bà Ngoại. "But I don't have enough to buy you new clothes right now. We'll have to make do with patching them again."

That evening, after chores, Bà Ngoại and I sat on the balcony of our bedroom. As she stitched the seam back together, I went through her collection of rags, looking for fabric to use as another patch.

CHAPTER EIGHT
The Bully Lies

WHEN I GOT TO SCHOOL the next day, Chie'n was waiting for me. "You ripped my knapsack," he said.

"That's not even possible."

"You're going to have to pay for it," he said, taking the knapsack off his shoulders and showing me a tiny tear along one of the pockets. "This is a very expensive knapsack."

"You did that yourself," I said.

Chie'n yelled out, "You're buying me a new knapsack!"

I watched as he stomped away, feeling good about sticking up for myself, but when I turned to look for Trang, I saw Sen, my sister Loan's friend. She clutched her schoolbooks to her chest and her face was creased with worry. Once Chie'n was out of earshot, she came up to me and whispered, "Don't you know his father is with the police? You need to stay out of his way."

My heart sank. Now I knew why everyone at school was afraid of Chie'n. How was it that I never realized his father was a policeman?

After school that day, Chie'n followed me home. I tried to lose him by hiding in corners and taking a slightly different route. But each time I turned around, he was still there. By the time I reached our kitchen door, he was just a few steps behind me. I slipped inside and slammed the door on his face, my heart pounding.

He hammered on the door, shouting, "You ripped my knapsack. You're going to pay!"

My knees buckled, and I collapsed onto the kitchen floor, wheezing badly and gulping for breath.

"Who is that boy out there?" asked Bà Ngoại, sounding alarmed. "If Dì and Bác come home and hear all that shouting, they will be very angry with you."

I opened my mouth, but all that came out was a spasm of coughs.

Bà Ngoại opened the door and Chie'n fell in. "Who are you?" she asked.

"My name is Pham Chie'n," he said, righting himself as he stepped inside. "You may know my father, who is Pham Bao, the policeman."

"It is good to make your acquaintance," said Bà Ngoại. "How can I help you?"

"That girl, Van," he said, pointing at me. "She ripped my knapsack. She needs to pay for it."

Bà Ngoại turned to me, a stormy look in her eye. "You should not have done this," she said.

I scrambled to my feet and tried to still my coughs, to talk over my wheezing. But no words came out. I shook my head, hoping that Bà Ngoại would understand that Chie'n was lying.

"Wait here, young man, I'll be back in a minute," she said.

Chie'n stood there, a smug look on his face as he sized up the kitchen. "Nice house," he said.

Bà Ngoại came back to the room with paper bills and coins. "This is all I have," she said, thrusting it into the boy's hands. "I am just a poor old woman."

I thought maybe that when Chie'n realized he was taking money from poor people, he would feel guilty. But he looked at what she'd given him and said, "This isn't enough for a new knapsack."

Bà Ngoại's face went still. "It has taken me years to save that."

Chie'n shoved the money into his pocket. "Fine. And because I'm a nice person, I won't tell my father about what Van did."

As the door closed behind him, Bà Ngoại turned to me, her hands on her hips. "You have brought dishonor to this family," she said. "Go and do your chores."

CHAPTER NINE
I Wish

BÀ NGOẠI'S WORDS cut me with their sharpness. Why wouldn't she take my side? Surely, she realized that Chie'n had been bullying me. I longed to explain what had happened, but my lungs still hurt with every breath. And even if I *had* been able to speak, talking back to Bà Ngoại when she was already angry was not a good idea.

I dragged myself up the stairs, feeling the weight of the world on my shoulders. Before starting my chores, I took some of my medicine and vomited up phlegm in the basin. I was lightheaded and weak by the time I spit out the last bit of phlegm.

I was too ashamed that night to eat supper. Would Bà Ngoại tell Dì and Bác what had happened? Would they punish me, or even kick me out of the house? Even though I already felt weak, I took extra care to clean their bedroom perfectly. When I was finished, I went to the third floor to be by myself. As always, it was hot up there, and I was sweaty from dusting and cleaning. I dragged a stool over to the balcony and stepped onto it, resting my arms on the edge of the concrete balcony wall. A bit of cool breeze brushed my face, and I almost wept. It reminded me of Ma's light kisses on my cheeks.

If Ma had been here, she would have protected me from Chie'n. She wouldn't have blamed me for something that wasn't my fault.

I gazed at the vast horizon of clay-tiled rooftops tinged orange in the setting sun and wondered about all the people who lived in the houses below. So many people. I wondered if anyone else felt as alone as I did.

Just then, Bà Ngoại came in, a steaming bowl of rice in her hands. She set it down and walked over to the balcony.

"What are you thinking, little one?" she asked.

"About Ma," I said.

"See all that sky?" asked Bà Ngoại, pointing beyond the clouds. "The ocean is out there. And farther away, Canada. You will go to Canada too, when you're older, and you'll be with your Ma and the rest of your family. We'll both go together."

I squinted to get a better look, but all I could see were the rooftops and sky. I wanted to believe Bà Ngoại that Canada was out there, and Ma too, but it didn't seem real.

"I'll sit while you eat," said Bà Ngoại, helping me down from the stool.

I settled in beside her at the counter by the sink, and she pushed the bowl of rice, aromatic with shrimp and vegetables, in front of me. With a shrimp poised between my chopsticks, I looked up at Bà Ngoại and said, "I miss Ma so much."

Bà Ngoại didn't say anything for minute or more but I could tell from the look on her face that she was angry. I popped the shrimp into my mouth and chewed slowly, waiting to hear what she would say.

"You need to be grateful for what you have."

It wasn't what I had expected. I swallowed the

shrimp, then set my chopsticks down. "I miss my family," I said. "I miss having clothing without patches. I wish I didn't have to work as a servant in this house. I wish I had more friends."

"You have a roof over your head," said Bà Ngoại. "You have enough to eat. And you have *me*. Don't you realize that we have just survived a war, and that our side *lost*? You have no idea how lucky you are."

"But Ma left me," I said.

"Only so she can give you a better life in a country that won't see you as the enemy," said Bà Ngoại. "I would have loved a childhood like yours."

Her words brought me up short. "What do you mean?" I asked.

"Never mind," she said. "What's done is done."

She got up from the table and began sorting through the basket of rags. "Now that I have no money to buy you new clothes, I guess I'll have to find good rags to patch your old clothes."

"You were going to buy me new clothes?" My face felt hot with shame.

"It was to be a surprise," she said, setting aside pieces of cloth.

Bà Ngoại did everything she could for me. She was like a second mother. She had even planned on spending what little money she had on clothes for me. And what did I do in thanks? Nothing but grumble and feel sorry for myself.

I went over to her and wrapped my arms around her waist. "Bà Ngoại, I love you and I am sorry for complaining."

She didn't pull my hands away, but she didn't answer either. She just kept on sorting rags.

"And I'm sorry for making you give money to Chie'n," I added.

She paused in her sorting and sighed. "I know he picked on you," she said. "I know that. But his father is a policeman. He could cause trouble for your aunt and uncle. The military police are watching them because your father and mother escaped. They're watching me too. Please stay out of his way."

I didn't know how I would stay out of Chie'n's way. He was at my school, after all. And he was the one following *me*. "I will try," I told her.

That night, as I lay in bed and hugged my pillow, I wondered about my grandmother's childhood. I crawled in beside her and wrapped my arms around her waist. "Bà Ngoại," I whispered. "Can you tell me what it was like when you were my age?"

CHAPTER TEN
Family Slave

BÀ NGOẠI WAS SILENT for so long that I thought maybe she was asleep. But at last she said in a low voice, "My parents died when I was a little bit older than you."

"Died?" I shuddered.

"Yes. They were farm workers. Ba was injured and died of an infection. Ma got dengue fever."

"Who looked after you?"

"My older brother let me live with him, but he wasn't very happy about it. He treated me like the family slave. I had no bed, so I would curl up on the floor in the kitchen to sleep. I worked all day and didn't go to school.

I wasn't fed, but had to beg for scraps from the table."

Bà Ngoại's words broke my heart. I kissed her shoulder.

"When I was old enough, I escaped from my brother's house. I took any job I could get—washing clothes, working in fields. And then I married your grandfather. He was the love of my life, your grandfather. He grew up without a family too. But he was smart and hardworking, just like me, and we made a wonderful family and life together."

"So you were happy, then." I said.

"It was the happiest time of my life," she said. "I had seven children, although two died as babies. Three girls and two boys survived. But one day my husband and our sons went on a trip together. I never saw them after that."

"What happened?"

"The communists took them and shot them dead. My husband and my two boys."

Bà Ngoại was quiet for a few minutes. I could feel her silent weeping. I lay my head on her back and wept too.

"I didn't let the death of my sons and husband defeat me," said Bà Ngoại at last. "I had to raise your mother and her sisters. All my daughters married good men and had successful family businesses. But the communists took that away from them and they were almost killed. Your parents lost their house, their motor sales company, and all their savings."

"And that is why we live here with Dì and Bác," I said.

"Yes," she said. "They have this house, but they lost their savings and their business as well. They only started making the rice sacks after the war. They are barely able to pay for the house and for food."

"But Dì doesn't treat you like her ma. She treats you like a servant," I said.

Bà Ngoại turned and looked at me. "Dì and Bác are kinder than you give them credit for, little one," she said. "Look what they've lost, yet they shelter us. They feed us and give us a roof over our heads. And we have beds to sleep in. The communists are now our government. Don't you see how much Dì and Bác risk by helping relatives who are considered enemies of the people?"

Bà Ngoại's words made me think. I had been so focused on my own troubles that I hadn't really thought of anyone else.

Bà Ngoại kissed me on the top of my head. "Be thankful for what you *do* have, little one, instead of fretting about what you *don't* have. Now go to sleep."

I stayed there cuddled beside Bà Ngoại until I heard the snores that told me she was asleep. I crawled back onto my own mat and hugged my pillow again, grateful that I wasn't alone.

CHAPTER ELEVEN
Trang's grandmother

CHIE'N CONTINUED to tease and bully me. And he wasn't the only one to do it. But I thought of Bà Ngoại's tough childhood and what she was going through even now. Could I be as strong as she was?

I could try.

As the days and weeks slipped by, I would look up at the clouds when kids at school said mean things. And I was thankful for Trang's friendship.

Then one day in late fall, Trang didn't come to school. She wasn't there the next day either. When she finally came back on the third day, I asked, "Have you been sick?"

She shook her head. "My grandmother fell," she said. "Her ankle was so swollen that she couldn't walk, so I had to do her work at the restaurant."

"Your bà ngoại works in a restaurant?" I asked.

"We *live* in a restaurant," said Trang. "Or behind it, to be exact."

"Your whole family?" I asked.

"Ma is dead," she said. "And Ba escaped by boat. Bà Ngoại and I live in the storeroom of the 99 Excellent Café. Bà Ngoại washes the dishes and I help her keep the kitchen clean. In exchange, they give us food and a place to sleep."

How was it that we had been friends for all these months and I never knew about her family? I guess because I didn't want to talk about mine, I never asked about hers.

"My family escaped by boat," I told her.

"I heard that your brother and sisters disappeared last spring," she said. "And I wondered if they'd escaped. Is your Ba dead?"

"No," I said. "He and my oldest sister Linh escaped when I was three."

"So, everyone's gone except you and your

grandmother?" she asked.

I nodded.

"I guess we're the same. The ones who were left behind."

Soon it was December. The dryer weather made it easier on my lungs. Was I happy? No.

But I became an expert at hiding my sadness.

CHAPTER TWELVE
From Canada

"Van, come downstairs!" called Bác.

I clutched the broom. What was Bác angry about now? I had managed to spin *more* yarn than usual this morning, and I had arrived home from school in good time, starting on my chores immediately. I quickly finished sweeping the last corner of Dì and Bác's bedroom floor and put the broom away.

I dragged my feet downstairs, dreading the confrontation. But he stood at the bottom of the stairs with a grin on his face and a pair of scissors in his hand. "Come to the living room," he said.

I followed him through my work area to the front

room of the house.

Perched on the gleaming black enamel coffee table was a huge battered-looking cardboard box. It was tied with string, and a rainbow of stamps were affixed to the top righthand corner. Bà Ngoại sat on a chair beside Dì, and they were both smiling.

"The box is from Canada," Bà Ngoại said. "From your father and mother."

"Ma sent this?" I asked, overwhelmed at the thought.

"She did," said Bác. "And now that we're all here, we can open it."

He snipped the string and carefully cut through the tape on the top of the box. I leaned in as he opened the flaps. Inside was a bunch of rectangular packages, each wrapped in newspaper, covered in words I couldn't read. On top of all the packages was an envelope addressed to Dì. She ripped the envelope open and removed a sheet of paper.

A photograph fell out of the envelope. I picked it up and gasped. It was a picture of my whole family—except for me. Ma had a huge grin on her face, and she stood beside a man who had to be Ba. Lined up in front of them were Tuan, Lan, and Loan. An older girl was with them too. She had to be my oldest sister Linh. They were all smiling.

The photograph made me happy and angry all at once. I was relieved that my whole family was safe. But why did they look so pleased? Didn't they miss me? Did they even *think* about me at all? I clutched the picture to my chest and forced myself to breathe slowly so I wouldn't cry.

"Let us all see the photograph," said Bà Ngoại, gently tugging it from my hand. Her index finger caressed the image of Ma.

Dì unfolded the paper and read aloud:

Dear Family,
    Please know that we are all safe.
    Van, my dear daughter. We love you and miss you. We are looking forward to the day when you will be with us again. In the meantime, please be obedient.

It was as if Ma's words had reached out and squeezed my heart. I could hardly breathe, I was so overwhelmed. We would be *together* again? Everyone kept telling me this, but how would it happen—and when?

The letter continued:

Dear Sister and Brother, thank you for caring for Van as if she were your own daughter. Our journey across the sea was filled with danger, and at times we worried that we would not survive. We live in a Canadian city called Saskatoon now. It is very cold, but my dear husband Nam laughed when I told him this, because he says that soon it will get even colder. In the winter it snows here. I am looking forward to seeing and touching snow, although it's hard to imagine weather colder than today. Even now, we must wear coats and shoes when we go outside.

The thought of Ma in such a place sent a shiver up my spine. Would the weather make her sick?

"Phuoc wrote to you too, Ma," said Dì to Bà Ngoại. "Here's what she says:

Ma, we are looking forward to the day when you and Van will join us in Canada. We have sent in the application to the government. Now we must wait. In this box are gifts for everyone. We love you and miss you.

Nam and Phuoc."

Bác reached in and took out the first package. He ripped off the newsprint to reveal a cellophane-wrapped box. He shook it and frowned, then held it up to his nose and sniffed. "I think I know what this is," he said, tearing off the cellophane. He removed the top of the box and grinned. "Chocolates."

He passed the box around and we each took one chocolate. Dì closed the box and put it in a cupboard.

I bit into my chocolate and savored the white gooey filling. It was such a treat to have something so sweet. And to think that it came all the way across the ocean!

The next package contained a beautiful red cotton t-shirt that looked about my size. Ma hadn't forgotten me! I could hardly wait to wear such a perfect shirt to school. Maybe then, the other students wouldn't make fun of me.

But Bác took it. "The police have been giving me trouble," he said, looking at me. "One has a daughter close to your age. I can give this to him, and maybe he'll leave us alone for a bit."

Bác opened several more packages containing a cotton t-shirt in a vibrant green, a pair of shorts, and a pair of trousers. He kept most of these too. Then Bác unwrapped a pair of blue jeans with a pink butterfly embroidered on the back pocket. My heart did a flip. They looked to be the perfect size for me. A few kids at school had blue jeans, but no one had blue jeans with a pink butterfly on the pocket.

"It's your lucky day," said Bác, tossing them into my lap. "They don't look like they'd fit anyone but you."

He continued opening packages. I got a pair of cotton shorts and a pale blue and mauve t-shirt. Bà Ngoại got a cotton blouse and new slippers.

That night, I tucked the photograph of my family underneath my pillow and dreamt that they were here with me.

CHAPTER THIRTEEN
What I Have

PACKAGES BEGAN to arrive from Canada every few months. I looked forward to hearing Ma's letters read out loud and I loved seeing photographs of my family. I was grateful that they were safe and that they all looked happy. But my life didn't change.

I didn't understand what Ma and Ba meant when they said that Bà Ngoại and I would be joining them. How could we do that? I imagined the two of us escaping in the middle of the night through the streets then onto a boat like Ba had done with Linh and Ma had done with Tuan, Lan, and Loan. How could that happen? Bà Ngoại's legs were too old to run, and my lungs were too weak.

A bit later in her letters, Ma wrote that we would be in an airplane. I had seen them up in the sky sometimes on my way to school. But how would we get inside one? She never explained that part.

Whenever I was sad or felt sorry for myself after this, I thought about what it was like for Bà Ngoại when she was my age. My life was so much better than hers had been. Trang was my friend, I had enough food to eat, and I had a grandmother who loved me.

And getting letters, photographs, and clothes from my family was better than having no family at all.

The months slipped by and I was six now. But each day seemed much the same as the day before. Trang was still my only friend at school. But as Bà Ngoại pointed out, one good friend is all anyone needs. Sometimes Trang would come to our place on a Saturday and we'd do our homework on the balcony or play a game. Other times, we'd meet at the schoolyard after we had both finished our chores and we'd toss a ball or shoot elastics. It was almost like having a sister.

But one thing we never did was meet at her place.

One day, Trang had been away for a whole week. I was worried, so I got her homework assignments from the teacher. I walked down the street the way I had seen Trang come to school so many times.

I found the 99 Excellent Café exactly where she had described it. It was a small restaurant. Most of the tables were empty except for one, where an elderly man ate a steaming bowl of *bún chả*. A tired looking woman, her hair combed into a high bun, was wiping down the counter with a dishrag. I approached her and asked, "Please, Missus, can you tell me where to find Vong Trang or her grandmother?"

The woman, who looked bored, hardly glanced at me. "Their place is right behind here. You can get to it through the alley. The gray door."

I turned into the alley with some misgivings. It looked exactly like the kind of place that Bà Ngoại was always telling me to avoid, but I needed to see Trang. I stepped through the mud, trying to avoid the garbage-filled puddles and clouds of flies. I held my breath against the stench of rotting fish, then knocked on the door several times before it cracked open and Trang peered out.

"What are you doing here?" she said, a look of panic in her eyes.

"I was worried about you," I answered.

For a minute I thought she was going to close the door in my face, but then I heard a voice from inside. "Is that your friend? How nice of her to visit."

Trang reluctantly opened the door wide and gestured for me to step inside. The room was tiny, with a rough concrete floor. It had the stale smell of old wok oil, but it didn't stink like the alleyway. There was a wooden table made from an oak barrel and a couple of wooden cartons as makeshift stools. A woman lay on a bamboo bed in the corner, bundled in ragged blankets, even though the room was stifling. And that was all. Not even a second bed. Trang and her grandmother must have to share.

"I'd like you to meet Bà Ngoại," said Trang, grabbing my hand and leading me to the side of the bed.

The old woman's eyes sparkled with intelligence and her face crinkled into a smile. "It is so nice to finally meet Trang's best friend," she said, reaching out a gnarled hand from under the covers. "I kept telling her she should bring you here."

I was surprised at the strength of her grip. "It's good to meet you too, honorable madam," I said, bowing in deference.

"Trang is fine," said her grandmother. "She's been looking after me and doing my work in the restaurant."

"Are you feeling better?" I asked.

"It's just a cold, but at my age it takes the wind out of me. Trang will be back at school on Monday." She propped herself up and rearranged the blankets. "Sit," she said, gesturing toward the table. "It will be nice for Trang to talk to a young person for a change."

I perched on the edge of one of the wooden crates and Trang sat across from me, her eyes cast down. "This place isn't as nice as yours," she said. "But it's our home."

"At least you don't have Dì and Bác to order you around," I said.

Trang smiled at that. "Madam Ky has her moods, but she's generally kind to us."

I opened my knapsack and took out the stack of assignments our teacher had given me. "Some of these are due on Monday," I said. "I didn't want you to get zero on them."

We chatted for a bit and then Trang's grandmother said, "Why don't you walk Van home? The fresh air will do you good."

Trang's face brightened. "Are you sure you'll be okay without me?" she asked.

"I'm nearly better," said her grandmother. "Now, go stretch your legs."

We walked in silence for nearly a block. At last Trang spoke up. "Do you still like me as a friend?"

Her question surprised me. "Why wouldn't I?"

"Because we're so poor."

"What difference does that make? I like you because you're a nice person."

"But you get clothes from Canada and you live in a big house. You could probably make other friends."

I was silent for a moment, thinking about her question. Then I said, "If someone wanted to be my friend just because I had clothes from Canada, they'd be a pretty boring friend."

Trang grinned at that. "I guess you're right," she said.

I visited Trang at her home from time to time after that, and I told Bà Ngoại about how nice Trang's grandmother was. "Tell Trang to bring her grandmother with her sometime when she visits you," said Bà Ngoại. "I'd love the company."

It didn't happen often, because both grandmothers had so much work to do, but they did get together sometimes to chat and laugh over cups of tea.

CHAPTER FOURTEEN
Fathers and Sons

ONE AFTERNOON after school, I arrived home and pushed open the kitchen door. Bà Ngoại was standing still, her eyes wide. Her knuckles, which clutched the edge of her apron, were white. A policeman stood facing her, a bored smirk on his face. I suddenly had a sinking feeling in the pit of my stomach.

The military police came frequently to question us and to search the house. But today was the worst possible day they could have chosen. We had just received a package from Ma yesterday and had opened it before bed. The package had contained money, plus items selected specially for Dì and Bà Ngoại to barter at the market. I wasn't sure if Dì had the time to hide every-thing because we had gone to bed so late.

"I know you've got money," the policeman said.

My heart nearly stopped beating. I kept my head down but looked at him through my lashes. It was Pham Bao, Chie'n the school bully's father. I had seen them on the street together last year. That man's voice was so familiar. Chie'n and his father even sounded alike.

Bà Ngoại took the small wooden box down from the cupboard above the sink, where she kept some money for the market. The rest of her cash was well hidden.

"I have this," she said, thrusting the box into his hands.

The policeman opened it, took out the few bills and coins, and stuffed them in his pocket. "You've got more than this," he said. "You got a package from Canada yesterday, didn't you?"

How did he know that? There must have been informers at the post office.

Pham Bao set the box on the counter and strode into the workroom. Bà Ngoại stayed where she was, as if planted to the kitchen floor. But I followed him.

He stopped in front of my spinning wheel and looked around the room, taking in the loom, the sewing table, and the huge mound of rice sacks.

"Quite the operation," he said. "This must bring in a good income."

He grabbed one of the rice bags and took it into the living room. He snatched the pillows off the sofa one by one and shook them, checking to see if anything was hidden inside. Then he checked behind the pictures on the wall and opened the drawers and cupboards. He found a box of chocolates with just a few candies missing.

"Only enemies of the people can afford sweets like this," he said, flashing a triumphant look my way. He gobbled a couple of the chocolates on the spot, then dumped most into the rice bag, tossing the almost-empty box on Dì's sofa.

One of the soft chocolates rolled out of the box and settled along the seam of the embroidered seat. It was sure to melt and stain. I ran to pick it up, but the policeman said harshly, "Leave it."

I followed behind helplessly as he climbed the stairs to the second floor. He tossed Dì and Bác's bedding onto the floor, looking for hidden valuables. He did find a green plastic necklace that Ma had sent to Dì, but this was just one from a whole box Ma had sent. Dì had kept this necklace for herself but was planning on bartering the rest. I had no idea where she had hidden the others. The policeman put the necklace in the rice bag, then went up to the third floor and tossed our bedding around as well.

He found the stash of family photographs I had hidden in my pillowcase. He flipped through them, frowning with disapproval. "All these people, your family—they're enemies," he said. "I should put the rest of you in prison."

He dropped the photos on the floor one by one and continued his search, going through Bà Ngoại's basket of rags and reading the labels on my medicine bottles. He didn't find much of interest.

By the time he left, the house looked like a water buffalo had gone through it. Yet he had found almost nothing of value. He hadn't discovered Bà Ngoại's secret stash of money, which she had hidden in the outhouse. And he hadn't found Dì's gold chains, which were stashed under the floor. All he took were some chocolates, a bit of grocery money, and a plastic necklace. But what a mess he made! I wondered if Dì and Bác would be angry with *me* when they got home.

I managed to get the front room back in order before they arrived. I missed supper that night because I was frantically cleaning their room before bedtime.

I was grumpy and tired all through school the next day. When I saw Chie'n at recess, I felt like yelling at him, but instead I just stomped around and frowned a lot. Trang began to wonder if I was angry at *her*.

On the day I turned eight, I realized with wonder that I was now taller than Bà Ngoại. Yet still our situation hadn't changed. When the packages and photographs arrived, it made me happy for a while. But that family across the ocean was like a storybook family now. They weren't real anymore. When they moved from Saskatoon to a place called Alliston, it didn't matter to me. Both places were still in Canada, so it seemed like no change at all.

I learned to cherish bits of happiness where I could find them—going to temple and the market with Bà Ngoại, and listening to her stories. There was comfort in that routine.

And Trang was still my best friend. There was comfort in that too.

CHAPTER FIFTEEN
Spinning Top

MONDAY, DECEMBER 2, 1985

"Look what I've got," said Trang that morning in the schoolyard. She opened her knapsack and I peeked inside. A bright green round plastic spinning top with a long string wound around it.

"How did you get *that*?" I asked. Chie'n had a spinning top, and one of his friends did too. At recess, kids would crowd around and watch. They would hold onto one end of the string, and, with a flick of the wrist, toss the top to the ground. If they did it just right, the top would spin, and the kids would cheer. It took a lot of practice to make a top spin. Trang and I would stay at the edge of the crowd. I longed to watch up close, but I didn't want Chie'n to notice me.

"A woman at the restaurant gave it to me when I was sweeping the floor," said Trang.

"That's wonderful," I said. "Can you make it spin?"

Trang threw her hands up in frustration. "I haven't even tried it yet. We don't have room for it at home."

"And Chie'n would probably steal it if you took it out here," I said.

"That's what I was thinking too."

"How about this," I said. "Let's wait until after school. Once Chie'n goes home, you can try it then."

Trang's eyes brightened. "Good idea."

After the final bell rang, I waited with her in the schoolyard. Some kids stayed around to play, but happily Chie'n wasn't one of them. When the schoolyard was nearly empty, we knelt side by side and Trang took the top out of her knapsack.

I watched with excitement as Trang tightened and straightened the string around the widest part of the round top. She looped the end of the string around her index finger, then flung the top forward. The string unrolled, but the top just clattered to the ground without even a single spin.

"Let me try," I said, holding out my hand.

Trang passed it over. I wound the string around the top and secured the end to two of my fingers. I flicked my wrist the way I had seen Chie'n do it, and tossed the top. It fell to the ground and bounced a few times. But it didn't spin.

"Give it back," said Trang. She tried throwing it from a standing position, but couldn't get it to spin either.

Back and forth we tried, but neither of us could get it to work. We were so focused on the top that I had no idea of how much time had passed until Mrs. Su stood over us.

"What are you girls still doing here?" she asked. "School has been out for over an hour. Your grandmothers are going to be worried."

Trang's head jerked up. "An *hour*? Oh no." She grabbed the top from the ground and stuffed it into her knapsack.

Trang and I followed Mrs. Su to the gate. As Trang turned left, I said, "I hope you don't get in trouble for being late."

"Bà Ngoại will be more worried than angry," she said.

I hurried home as fast as I could, not so much worried about my own bà ngoại as I was about Dì and Bác. What if they were already home? They would be furious with me for not getting the cleaning done. But even so, I was glad that I had stayed late with Trang. Even though we didn't get the top to spin, it was so fun trying. It was nice to play for a little while. I could hardly wait until tomorrow to try it again. We'd have to figure out a spot where we could practice with the spinning top without Chie'n noticing us.

I pushed the kitchen door open and stepped inside, prepared to be yelled at or punished.

"Van," said Bà Ngoại, enveloping me in her arms and kissing my cheeks.

This was not the greeting I expected.

"Hi, Bà Ngoại," I said. "Sorry that I'm late. I'll start on my chores right now."

"Your chores can wait," she said. "I have something to show you."

She grabbed my hand and led me to the staircase. "It's in our room."

An opened box from Canada sat on her bamboo bed. I looked in confusion from Bà Ngoại to the box. These packages had been arriving regularly over the past four years. Yes, it was nice to get them, but Bà Ngoại was acting as if this was something unusual.

I opened the flaps and reached inside, drawing out a long-sleeved blue jacket made of thick material that appeared to be my size. "This looks like a coat Loan was wearing in a photograph," I said.

"Try it on," said Bà Ngoại.

I drew my arms through the sleeves and did the zipper up the front. "I can't wear this," I said. "It's too hot."

"Take a look at what else is in the box," said Bà Ngoại.

I reached in and took out a bigger version of the coat in green. "This one must be for you," I said, handing it to Bà Ngoại.

At the bottom of the box were long heavy pants—a pair for each of us—and sturdy shoes that covered our whole foot up to our ankles. "What funny things Ma and Ba sent this time," I said. "Maybe they've been in Canada so long that they've forgotten how hot it is here."

"We'll be needing these clothes. We're going on a trip." Bà Ngoại handed me an opened envelope addressed to her in Ma's loopy handwriting. I pulled out the letter and unfolded it. Inside were several official-looking documents typewritten in English.

"What are these?" I asked, fanning the documents out in my hand.

"Airplane tickets to Toronto, Canada," she said. "And papers from the Canadian government that say we're allowed to go there."

"Tickets? Papers?" I asked. "What do you mean?"

Bà Ngoại grinned broadly. "We're *finally* moving to Canada. You'll be with Ma and Ba and Tuan, Linh, Lan and Loan."

"But they live in a place called Alliston, not Toronto," I said. None of this made sense.

"Toronto is the closest airport," said Bà Ngoại. "They will meet us there and take us to their home."

The thought of leaving everything familiar and traveling to be with people I didn't know terrified me. My chest felt tight with panic.

"Why don't we just stay here?" I asked. "This is our home."

"Our home is with our family," said Bà Ngoại.

"But Trang just got a spinning top," I said. "I don't know how to make it work yet."

Bà Ngoại looked bemused. "I am sure they have spinning tops in Canada."

My eyes filled with tears. My parents and siblings had faded in my memory. They didn't seem like real people anymore, just pictures on paper. But Trang was real, and so was the spinning top.

"What about temple?" I asked. "They don't have that in Canada. Or the market, or cyclos." I threw myself down on the bed and buried my face in my pillow. "I won't go."

Bà Ngoại sat beside me. I could feel the warmth of her hand as she caressed my back. "I know this is hard for you to think about," she said. "But we are going on this trip and you *will* be happy."

I knew better than to argue with Bà Ngoại, but I knew that she was wrong. How could I possibly be happy? Why couldn't we just both stay here? My whole life was here. I took some deep breaths and wiped the tears from my cheeks with the back of my hand. I got up from the bed. "I need to do my chores," I said angrily.

As I dusted and swept and cleaned, a stream of sweat trickled down my spine. Did people in Canada ever sweat? It was probably too cold for that. And what about fruit? It was probably too cold there to grow it. How would I ever get used to a country covered in snow and ice?

That night as I slept, I dreamed that I was on a boat, stuck in the middle of an ocean made of ice. No matter how hard I tried, I couldn't reach Canada. And no matter how hard I tried, I couldn't get the boat to go back home to Ho Chi Minh City.

I was in the middle of two worlds, shivering in a heavy coat and big shoes.

CHAPTER SIXTEEN
Learning a Trick

TRANG'S EYES filled with tears when I told her I was leaving for Canada the following week. "I'll miss you," she said. "But I'm also jealous."

Word spread around school that I would be leaving for Canada. It was as if suddenly, I was the most important person in the whole place. Kids from my class who hardly spoke to me before now wanted to be my friend. Even Chie'n greeted me with a smile.

"Why is everyone acting so strangely?" I asked Trang after the bell rang for recess.

"I'm not sure," she said. "I guess they think you're special now. Maybe they think you'll send them something from Canada."

"Are they really that shallow?" I asked. But even as I said it, I knew she was right. Kids were popular for the silliest of reasons. Now I worried about Trang. Who would be her friend after I was gone? But her comment gave me an idea.

"Bring your spinning top out for recess, okay?"

Trang looked at me oddly, "I don't want it to get stolen," she said.

"Trust me," I told her. "I have a plan."

She took the top out of her knapsack. Once we were outside, I grabbed her hand and pulled her over to where Chie'n and his friends were playing.

Chie'n had just thrown his top down, and it was doing a wobbly spin.

"Chie'n!" I called out.

He looked up with a frown. But when he saw it was me, his face broke into a smile. "Van," he said with false sincerity. "Nice to see you. Do you want to watch? You can stand right beside me."

"Actually," I said, "Trang has her own top and I was wondering if you could teach us how to make it spin."

Trang held out her spinning top.

"Wow," said Chie'n, taking her top in his hands and examining it. "This is a good one."

He wound the string tightly around the widest part of the top and twisted the loose end of the string around his knuckle. Then he flung the top down to the ground with a flick of his wrist. It clattered and stopped, without spinning even once.

His face looked stormy and I thought that I had made a huge mistake. Trang's eyes were round with worry. Then Chie'n took a breath and smiled at us both.

"This one must take a slightly different technique," he said.

He wound the string back around the top, then weighed the top in one hand, then the other. He didn't say anything, but concentrated in silence. Then he let it go again.

I was so afraid it would clatter and stop like before. Instead, it spun.

Perfectly.

Trang and I cheered. Chie'n grinned.

"Let me show you how to twist the string the right way," Chie'n said to Trang.

It was such a pleasure watching the two of them concentrate on perfecting the technique of spinning Trang's top. Their heads were so close together that they nearly touched. Trang wound the string the way Chie'n showed her and tried to fling it down with the same flick of the wrist. Over and over she tried, but it wouldn't spin. The bell rang and recess was over.

"It just doesn't work for me," she said, her voice cracking with frustration.

"It will," said Chie'n. "We'll practice at lunch, okay?"

During the lunch break, dozens of kids stood around and watched as Chie'n coached Trang. When she finally succeeded, their cheers were deafening.

I didn't learn how to do it myself because I didn't want to take the attention off Trang. She had to stay at this school. It was important that she have friends after I was gone.

CHAPTER SEVENTEEN
Handful of Cloud

WE INVITED Trang and her grandmother to come over for one last visit on the Sunday afternoon before we left. While the grandmothers had tea in the kitchen, Trang and I went up to the third floor.

"I have a surprise for you," I said, barely able to control my excitement. I pointed to the cardboard box from Canada, which sat on my bamboo bed.

"What's in it?" asked Trang, puzzled.

"Take a look."

Trang opened the flaps. On top was a red t-shirt and a pair of my shorts, barely worn.

"Is this what you're taking to Canada?" she asked.

"No," I said. "This is what I'm leaving behind—for you."

Trang's eyes filled with tears. "*Really*? But why?"

"The weather is different in Canada," I said. "Ma sent me and Bà Ngoại some Canadian clothes that we're supposed to wear on the airplane. Other than that, Ma told us that we're just to take a change of underwear and my medicine."

Trang threw her arms around me. "It's so nice of you to give these to me," she said. "Now, every time I wear them, I'll think of you."

I still wasn't used to the idea of leaving my life behind and starting on a journey. But it felt good to know that Trang would have friends at school and nicer things to wear.

Side by side we stood at the balcony, looking beyond the houses where the sky met the earth. "That's how far away you'll be," she said. "I'm going to miss you."

"I'm going to miss you too," I said. "And I'm also scared."

"Of what?"

"Right at this minute? Mostly, of the airplane trip," I said, looking up into the sky.

Trang pointed at a particularly fluffy cloud. "You'll be up as high as that," she said. "I think that will be exciting." Just then, an airplane flew across the sky. It seemed to go right through the cloud.

"Maybe," she added, "when you're on your airplane, you can do me a favor."

"What?"

Trang chuckled. "Roll down the window and grab me a handful of cloud."

The thought made me giggle. "Wouldn't it be neat if I could?"

CHAPTER EIGHTEEN
Leaving Bác and Dì

THE FOUR OF US walked out the front door together. Bác stood in the street and flailed his arms. An automobile with a taxi sign on top swerved out of the traffic and screeched to a stop in front of the house. Bác opened the back door and held onto Bà Ngoại's elbow as she crouched down and stepped inside. In her arms, she clutched a zippered leather folder that held our important papers. I got in next, and Bác passed me the small suitcase, which carried only a change of underwear and my medicines. We were wearing our Canadian coats, pants and shoes, and already I was feeling uncomfortably warm. Dì scrambled in beside me, and Bác opened the front door and sat beside the taxi driver.

"We're going to the airport," he said.

The driver grunted in response and gunned the engine as he steered back into the middle of traffic.

I had never been in an automobile before. It felt strange, sitting between my aunt and grandmother. I sat up straight so I could look out the window and drink in the familiar sight of cyclos speeding by and pedestrians weaving in and out. This was the last time I would see the streets of Ho Chi Minh City.

What did streets look like in Canada? I wondered.

The taxi stopped in front of a long modern-looking building that seemed to be just two storeys tall and we all got out, but the taxi idled.

Dì put a piece of paper in my hand. "This is your parents' telephone number and their names written in English," she said. "When you get to Canada, show it to someone in case of emergency." She hugged me tight, then held me at arm's length. "I will miss you, dear Van," she said, her eyes brimming with tears.

I was surprised. I shocked myself by hugging her back. "I'll miss you too," I said. And I meant it.

Bác stood beside her, his hands in his pockets and a serious look on his face. "Do not let go of Bà Ngoại's hand in the airport," he said. "You don't want to lose each other."

"Thank you for letting us live with you," I said formally.

Bác looked stern at first, but then he smiled. "Safe travels," he said.

We watched them get back into the taxi and waved as they drove away. I felt empty and strange and frightened, standing there. I clutched the flimsy suitcase in one hand and gripped Bà Ngoại's hand with the other. My old life had just disappeared.

Bà Ngoại shoved the zippered leather folder inside of her top, and I carried our suitcase. When we stepped inside the building, Bà Ngoại seemed confused for a moment. She approached a man in a uniform and showed him our tickets.

"Go that way," he said, pointing to a lineup at the far end of the building.

Dozens of people were waiting in front of an officer in a glass booth. We stepped in behind the last one. When it was our turn, Bà Ngoại showed him our papers and tickets. He asked her some questions. He looked down at me and smiled. With a loud *bang*, he stamped our papers and waved us through. We walked down a hallway, and then stood in another lineup. This happened a few more times, but finally we were directed to wait in a room with a floor-to-ceiling window that looked out over the runway, which looked like a long, wide road.

I pressed my face against the window and watched in awe as airplanes took off and landed in front of me. I had never seen an airplane up close. I had no idea that they were so huge. And I realized that they had to be very heavy with all that metal and so many people and luggage inside. How did they manage to stay in the air?

At last I was able to see how you got inside. Once an airplane came to a stop, a door would open from inside. When the door was pushed down, it became a set of stairs. I watched people walk down them. Soon, others walked up the stairs and disappeared inside.

A uniformed woman made an announcement through a microphone. Bà Ngoại said, "That's us."

We followed a snaking lineup outside and onto the

apron of the runway. And then it was our turn to walk up those steps and into the airplane.

The inside looked like a tidy classroom with seats instead of desks. With all the people and all the seats, it seemed far too solid to lift into the air. I didn't want to worry Bà Ngoại, however, so I didn't say anything. Our seats were side by side near the front, and mine was by the window.

When the plane took off, I held my breath and clutched Bà Ngoại's hand. I hoped and prayed that the airplane wasn't too heavy. At first all I could hear was a loud grinding, whirring noise. It felt as if we were going straight up in the air. But after a few minutes, the whirring sounded more like a hum and we leveled out. Now we seemed to be floating. I opened my eyes and looked out the window. Down below, the buildings of Ho Chi Minh City looked like toys. Beside me, the clouds were so close that I felt I could touch them. Of course, the windows didn't roll down—and even if they did, how could I catch a cloud for Trang? But the thought made me smile.

I don't remember much more about flying to Canada. It was a long trip and I slept through most of it. I have a vague memory of Bà Ngoại waking me up so we could switch planes, and then sitting in another airport somewhere. I remember eating vegetables and rice from a small square container on one airplane, and some sort of noodles on another. The bathroom in the airplane was white and clean, with no spiders. The little room had a basin with running water in it and even a spout where soap came out. I could have stayed in that bathroom for a long time, just trying to figure it all out. But someone knocked on the door, so I had to leave.

We flew all through the day and night and into another day. Finally, the pilot announced that we were about to land in Toronto.

Bà Ngoại and I clutched hands as the airplane bumped to the ground and taxied down the runway. It shuddered to a halt in front of a big building. We had taken off our heavy coats and big shoes, but now we scrambled into them again and did them up tight. The doors opened, and we lined up with the other passengers to exit.

My heart pounded with anticipation. Would Ma be waiting for me on the other side of the door? Would she finally hold me in her arms and tell me that she loved me and missed me? It was almost too much excitement to handle.

When we walked through the airplane doors, we were inside a tunnel instead of outdoors. Even so, I could feel the bite of cold air seeping in through the walls. I was thankful for my heavy coat and big shoes, but I shivered all the same.

At the end of the tunnel, we followed the other people. We had to get through more lineups to show officers our papers and answer their questions. It was almost exactly like when we left Vietnam.

"When are we going to see Ma?" I asked Bà Ngoại.

"Soon," she said as she pulled out Ma's letter. "We just have to follow what everyone else does. Once we're through security and customs, we'll be able to leave the airport. See what she writes here? Your ma says they will all be waiting for us once we go through the exit. They'll be holding a sign for us, so we can see them right away."

I looked around the big room and saw that there was indeed a door that had the letters Ma described—EXIT— over top in big, red letters. We had one more officer to talk to, and then we would be through.

I waited patiently, thinking about how it would feel to see Ma again after so many years. It had been so long since I had seen Ba that I couldn't imagine him at all. I was looking forward to seeing Tuan and my sisters. But mostly, I just wanted to hug Ma.

When Bà Ngoại finally got a chance to show that last officer our papers, I could barely contain my excitement. We were about to step through that door, and my life would change forever. But what if Ma didn't recognize me? What if I didn't recognize *her*?

The man and woman in front of us stepped through the door that said EXIT. We were right behind them. My heart fluttered at the sight of dozens of people waiting for their loved ones, waving signs in different languages, but mostly in Vietnamese. One sign said, *Welcome, Bao and Thi!* and another said, *Welcome to Canada, Khanh and Lac.*

I stood on my tiptoes and searched the signs. I couldn't find any that said, *Welcome, Van and Bà Ngoại!* Then I looked at the faces that held the signs. I tried to see if I could find Ma.

But I couldn't.

"Maybe they got held up," said Bà Ngoại.

We waited in that welcoming area and watched many people as they were reunited with their friends and family. One girl about the same age as I was ran and hugged a woman. "Ma, I missed you!" she cried.

Husbands met wives and fathers met sons. But no one came for us. My deepest fear seemed to be coming true. Were we left behind once again?

"I don't understand," said Bà Ngoại as the last passengers were greeted by loved ones and walked out of the airport together. "Your ma said they'd all be waiting for us. Maybe we're in the wrong place."

"How can we be in the wrong place?" I asked her. "We just followed everyone else. They were all met by someone. We're the only people who weren't."

"Do you still have that piece of paper that Bác gave you?" asked Bà ngoại.

I had forgotten all about it. I reached into my pocket and drew it out. "Here it is," I said, handing it to my grandmother.

"Now we just need to find a person to help us," said Bà Ngoại.

Only there wasn't any official looking person in this

part of the airport. "Let's sit and wait," I said, grabbing Bà Ngoại's hand and leading her to a bench. "Maybe they're just late."

We sat and waited for what seemed like hours. No one showed up for us. No one in a uniform came by. I could see that Bà Ngoại's hand held onto the handle of our suitcase with a white-knuckled grip.

"What about that lady?" I asked, pointing to a woman wearing an apron and mopping the floors.

"She's not an officer," said Bà Ngoại. "How could she help us?"

"But she's the only person we've seen," I said. "Why don't we show her the piece of paper and see what happens?"

I didn't want to lose Bà Ngoại, so when she approached the cleaner, I stayed right by her side. Bà Ngoại thrust the crumpled paper into her hands and said in Vietnamese, "We are lost."

The woman took the paper, then looked at us. She gazed over at the door we had come through. Even though she didn't speak Vietnamese, she seemed to understand what our problem was right away. She motioned for us to follow her.

"We can't leave here," I told Bà Ngoại. "Didn't Ma tell us to wait for them?"

"We'll come right back," said Bà Ngoại. "I think this woman may be able to help us."

The woman led us to an office down the hallway where there were desks and telephones and people looking busy. She talked to a woman with yellow hair, then showed her our piece of paper.

My heart pounded as I watched the woman pick up the telephone and call the number written on the piece of paper. She seemed to be speaking to many different people while Bà Ngoại and I stood there, wondering what was happening. Then, finally, she handed the telephone to Bà Ngoại.

"My daughter!" said Bà Ngoại, when she heard the voice on the other end. "Why aren't you at the airport? We've been waiting for hours."

I tried to make sense of the conversation, but I could only hear half of it. When Bà Ngoại finally hung up the phone, she grinned at me. "You'll never believe it—they had the wrong date."

"What?" I said. "After all these years, they couldn't remember the date we were coming to Canada?"

"It's not like that," said Bà Ngoại gently, wrapping one arm around my shoulder. "There is a date change between Vietnam and Canada. The date on our tickets is different than the dates they were given."

It seemed a strange excuse. I had a great sense of emptiness. I felt let down again. "Then when are they coming?" I asked.

"Your ba is at work right now," said Bà Ngoại. "Your ma is going to call Ba at work and have him come home immediately. He'll pick up your ma, sisters, and brother, and come here directly. That will take about two hours."

Bà Ngoại found a fountain and we both had some water to drink. I was too nervous to be hungry—it was just as well, because the food people were eating at the restaurant looked strange. Bà Ngoại was relieved when I said I didn't want anything.

"I'm not hungry either," she said.

Even if we had wanted to eat, we probably didn't have enough money. We didn't have Canadian money anyway.

We sat on a bench and huddled together. Soon I fell into a deep sleep.

CHAPTER NINETEEN
Streaks of Silver

I DREAMED that I was in a warm bed, surrounded by my sisters and brother. It felt so good to be hugged, to be loved. I felt like I was rocking back and forth, like a baby in a cradle.

"My baby, my Van! I can't believe I'm finally holding you."

The words seemed to be part of the dream at first. But I felt strong arms hugging me, holding me close. I opened one eye just a crack. A man. A stranger. Streaks of silver in his dark hair. Fine wrinkles on his face. He was holding me tight and weeping.

Was this Ba?

It couldn't be. My ba had a smooth face and black hair. He smelled of incense and soap. This man was old and he smelled of smoke and work.

This man frightened me. I squeezed my eyes shut and pretended to be asleep.

Something tickled my cheeks. I felt a warm face up against mine. "Van, my baby girl. Wake up."

Ma's voice.

I opened my eyes.

"You came for me!" I cried, squirming away from the old man so I could wrap my arms around Ma's neck. "I missed you so much."

Ma hugged me tightly, and the man who looked like a stranger let go of me.

I turned to him. He looked sad. "Are you my ba?" I asked. And he nodded. I reached over and hugged him too. "You look so different."

Suddenly, I was enveloped in a huge hug with many arms. There was Tuan, looking almost as tall as Ba, and Linh, looking like a grown woman. Loan had tears running down her face, and Lan was grinning broadly. They all tried to hold onto me at once.

"Where's Bà Ngoại?" I asked.

And then I saw her, standing to one side, just watching. And smiling.

"We have a long drive home," said Ma. "And you're going to be cold."

She gave me and Bà Ngoại each a wool hat and a pair of mittens.

When we stepped out of the building, the air was so cold that it hurt my lungs. How did people live in temperatures like this? It was the middle of the night and the sky was black, but I gasped when I looked up high. "What are those sparkling things?" I asked.

"Those are stars," said Tuan. "You can see them here on clear nights."

We had talked about stars in school, but in Ho Chi Minh City the sky was hazy, so I had never seen a star for myself. I shivered as the icy wind cut through my coat and hat and gloves.

"The car is just over here," said Ba, leading the way.

The car was very much like the taxi, but a bit bigger. All of us kids piled into the back and Bà Ngoại sat in the front with Ma and Ba. As Ba navigated out of the parking lot and onto the road, I looked out the window. I was amazed at how wide the road seemed.

"Where are all the people?" I asked.

"This is a highway," said Ba. "No one walks on it or takes a bicycle on it. Only cars and trucks use it."

I leaned forward so I could see through the front windshield. A whole line of cars were coming toward us with their lights on. Up above, giant lamps illuminated the road. I stared out the window, marveling at the huge lit-up billboards and big metal structures.

I could feel my eyes getting heavy, but I was too excited to sleep. I tried to answer the questions that Tuan and my sisters asked me. But their Vietnamese sounded strange, and they kept on adding in English words that I couldn't understand. I didn't mind. As we drove on, I relished the warmth of my siblings' legs and shoulders. We leaned into each other and I enjoyed the buzz of their chatter. In the front seat of the car, Bà Ngoại smiled and talked. She looked so much younger when she was happy.

My eyes had just closed when Ba slowed the car down and pulled into a driveway. He turned to me and said, "Van, you are now home."

When I climbed out of the car, I looked down at

the ground. It was white, and as I stepped on it, I could see my shoe prints. "Is this snow?" I asked.

"It is," said Tuan. "Look up to the sky."

I stood as still as I could and looked up. The snow was like slow-moving dots. I held out my hand and caught one on my mitten, then held it up close. It wasn't a dot at all, but a tiny perfect star. It reminded me of how Trang and I joked about catching a cloud. Were clouds made up of thousands of snowflakes?

Maybe I had just caught my first cloud.

CHAPTER TWENTY
A Bed for Sisters

I FOLLOWED my family up the stairs to the second
floor of the building. Ba unlocked the door to our
apartment and opened it wide. It was black inside,
but Ba went in first. I heard a click, and the room was
illuminated as if it were daylight.

I stepped inside. The room was huge.

Red velvet chairs and a sofa faced a giant television
box. I knew the box was called a television because Dì
and Bác had purchased one just two years ago and it
sat in their bedroom.

I stepped out of my big shoes and felt the softness
of the carpet through my socks. "Take a look at the

kitchen," Ma said, grabbing my hand and pulling me forward. "That's a refrigerator for storing food," she said, pointing to a large green metal cabinet. "And that's a stove to cook with," she said, pointing to a shorter metal cabinet that was painted white. "We have electricity, so no need to use coal. And with the refrigerator to keep food fresh, Bà Ngoại won't have to go to the market every day."

I was led from room to room. It took me a while to take it all in. "Do you know what a television does?" Tuan asked me with a grin.

I shrugged. As far as I knew, it was just a fancy box that I had to dust every day when I lived with Dì and Bác.

Tuan turned a knob on the box, and suddenly lights and shapes flicked behind the glass. I stood, mesmerized, as the dancing shapes settled into images of people walking and talking inside the little box. Bà Ngoại sat down on the sofa. She couldn't take her eyes off the images.

"Are you hungry?" asked Tuan. "We didn't get supper because we were in such a rush to reach you."

I followed him into the kitchen. He took out some

bowls and spoons, and set a big box on the table.

"It's not much of a first meal in Canada," he said. "But I love this cereal." He filled up two bowls with crispy small yellow balls from the box. Then he grabbed a carton from the refrigerator.

"What is that?" I asked, pointing to the carton.

"Milk," he said.

"It's *cold*?" I asked.

He nodded. "I like it, but it has a different taste from what you're used to."

He poured milk on top of the cereal, and then pushed one bowl and spoon over to my side of the table. He ate a spoonful of the mixture and swallowed it down.

"Try it," he said.

I dipped my spoon into the strange mixture, retrieving a single ball and a bit of cold milk. I put it in my mouth.

"Yuck!" I dropped the spoon back into the bowl.

"You'll get used to it," Tuan said, grinning. "I really like it now."

Since I couldn't remember the last time I had eaten, I decided to have a few more spoonfuls of the stuff. Maybe all Canadian food tasted this bad. I'd just have to get used to it.

There were other things that were going to be easier to get used to, like the bathroom. The toilet was even nicer than the one in the airplane. There was a sink like the airplane bathroom as well, with hot and cold water, and a mirror above. But best of all was a huge white enamel tub.

"It has hot and cold water just like the sink," said Linh, stepping in the tub as I stood staring at it. "You can fill the whole thing up with water to bathe in instead of just using a cup at a time."

The flat also had four bedrooms. One was for Ma and Ba to sleep in. The smallest bedroom was Tuan's. Bà Ngoại got her very own bedroom, but I shared with my three sisters. It held two beds that were raised off the floor and had mattresses instead of bamboo mats. The two beds were pushed together so it was like the four of us were sleeping in one giant bed.

When we finally went to bed that night, I was too excited to sleep. I savored the warmth of my sisters surrounding me. I thought of Ma and Ba so close that only a wall separated us, not an ocean and sky. Tuan was just a wall away too, and I could hear Bà Ngoại's light snores from her room.

I was still scared about leaving behind everything that was familiar. I was not sure about Canadian food or the snow. It bothered me that I couldn't understand everything my family talked about. I knew it would take a long time to learn English and to get used to this new way of life. But I didn't care. For the first time since I was three years old, my whole family was together again.

Nobody was left behind.

And Canada was home.

TOO YOUNG TO ESCAPE
Author's Note

I OFTEN do school presentations of *Adrift at Sea*, my picture book about Tuan Ho, who escaped Vietnam by boat with his mother and his older sisters when he was six. His little sister Van (who is now known as Vanessa) was too young to make the dangerous journey, I explain. So she was left behind. Immediately one urgent question comes up time and again: *What happened to Van?*

Kids could not imagine how awful it must have been for her to wake up one morning and discover that her mother and siblings had escaped in the middle of the night without explaining why or even kissing her good-bye. I was obsessed with this question as well, so I approached Vanessa with the idea of a book—a chance for her to tell her side of the story.

She agreed.

I was spellbound as Vanessa told me about the spindle; the spiders in the outhouse; the bully at school; and her one true friend. But it's not an easy thing to build a narrative using a grown woman's recollections of a time when she was only four. There were naturally gaps in her memory, and many small details were lost. As well, Van recalled incidents, but not what happened immediately before or after. As I wrote, I filled in details using clues from her memories and my own research and imagination. I would write the draft, then pass it back to Vanessa. She would read it, then share it with her parents and siblings. Later, she'd get back to me with clarification and more details.

One thing that initially bogged me down was the fact that there were many extended family members living in her aunt and uncle's house while she was there. These others didn't play a significant role in the narrative, but I was confronted with a choice: do I develop each of these relatives as their own character with interaction with Van? Or do I simply leave them out? My first draft was filled with references to each of these family members, but the narrative felt cluttered and confusing. For the sake of clarity, I took out the family members who didn't play an essential role in Van's narrative.

I have deep admiration for Vanessa's father and mother, who were faced with the toughest choice that parents could make. I also admire Van's aunt and uncle, who were put in a difficult situation. Over time, they gave refuge to extended family; and they did it under the nose of the communist regime at great risk to themselves. I especially admire Vanessa's grandmother. Everyone should have a grandmother like Bà Ngoại. Her strength and love buoyed Van up in her darkest days.

And, Vanessa, I thank you for sharing your story. I realize that my questions were sometimes probing and relentless, but I wanted the world to see you the way that you are—a remarkable woman who is loving and forgiving and strong and generous, and so very cherished by her parents and siblings.

–M. F. S.

An interview with Van's Father, Nam Ho

You left Vietnam in 1980. What would have happened to you if you had stayed in Ho Chi Minh City?

I was in the Army Republic of Vietnam (ARVN), which meant that I was fighting for South Vietnam. The communists were fighting with North Vietnam, and they won. After the communists took over Vietnam, members of the ARVN were treated like enemies. Under the communists, I was not allowed to work or own my own home. I was in danger of being sent to a so-called camp for reeducation about communism. These camps were actually prisons, and inmates could be held for many years before they were finally released. I had to escape so that my family would have the freedom to live. If we had stayed, I am afraid to think of what our lives would have been like.

How did it feel to leave your wife and younger children behind for so long?

It was the most terrifying and difficult decision of my life—a decision I had to make in a matter of days. In the end, I resolved to risk everything for a better life and a future for my children.

What did you think of Canada when you arrived?

From the second Linh and I landed here in 1980, everyone wanted to help us adjust to this very different country. We were offered clothing, shelter, and generosity. I will be forever grateful to the Canadians who helped us out. Without their kindness, I'm not sure what would have happened.

What did you do for work, and how did you get the rest of your family to Canada?

As soon as I arrived, I looked for employment. My first job was as an apartment handyman. I did whatever job they asked me to do: mowing lawns, cleaning carpets, shoveling snow. Working hard helped me adjust to life in Canada. Within two weeks of finding a job, I started the long process of sponsoring my family to come to Canada. It could take years. In May 1981, my wife decided they could not wait in Vietnam. She escaped with Loan, Lan, and Tuan. They landed in a refugee camp in Malaysia. I then changed the paperwork to sponsor my wife and children from that refugee camp.

How did you keep in contact with your family during the long separation?

Communication was challenging in the early eighties. Phones were not common in Vietnam, and there wasn't one in the home where Van lived. If we wanted to have a phone conversation, we had to arrange a time in advance by mail or telegram, and Van and her grandmother would go to a phone center to make the call.

It was hard to keep in contact by mail because letters were opened and read by the communist government. Letters that criticized communism or life in Vietnam would not be delivered. Letters also couldn't contain positive information about life outside of Vietnam. We had to be very careful about what we wrote so that our loved ones left in Vietnam didn't get into trouble.

What were your thoughts when you finally held Van in your arms for the first time after all those years?

I was overwhelmed with emotion. Tears flowed like a river. Five years had passed. She was three years old when I left, and here she was, a little lady. She was so very thin and frail. I was happy that our family was finally reunited. We were lucky. Not all families in similar situations had a happy ending like ours.

What else would you like readers to know?

I want them to know about the importance of family. Cherish your family every day, and never take them for granted. Tell your children you love them, and hug them as though you won't have another chance to hug them again. Love them unconditionally and they will reciprocate.

An interview with Van's Mother, Phuoc Ho

Why were you forced to leave Van behind?

Freedom. For the sake of my children and their future, staying in Vietnam was not an option. Canada offered opportunities and a bright future. I had to do it for them.

We had five children. My husband took our eldest daughter, Linh, during his escape. My original plan was to escape with my four children. Loan was ten, Lan was eight, Tuan was six, and Van was four.

Days before we were to leave, I was told I couldn't take all four children. The journey was dangerous, and

I would have to run across fields and ponds with the police chasing us. Tuan and Van were both so young that they would have to be carried. I could not carry both.

My sister understood my terrible dilemma. She offered to take care of Van until I could sponsor her and my mom to Canada.

What were your thoughts as you left Van sleeping on that night that you escaped?

I was devastated and heartbroken. What mother leaves her child behind? I was worried about Van and how she would live without me, but I had to make the very difficult decision to leave. This was for all my children's future. Our lives were at risk. I placed my trust in my sister to take good care of Van and Mom.

We left at night. Van was sleeping peacefully, and my tears poured as I thought how very different life was going to be for her the next morning. She had no idea we were leaving and would have a hard time understanding. I felt an incredible rush of regret. Was I making the right decision? How could I leave my four-year-old daughter? How bad could it be if we stayed?

I couldn't hug her good-bye for fear that it would wake her. I left sobbing, whispering under my breath that we would be reunited in the future.

What was it like during those years when you were separated from Van?

My children and I quickly adjusted to life in Canada. I found a job right away. I had to start making money to send home, so that my sister and mom could take care of Van.

Not a day went by when I didn't think of Van. My heart ached, wondering how she was doing. I worried about whether she was being properly taken care of and whether she was eating enough—in her pictures she looked very thin. Sometimes I worried that she'd forget me. Other times I was afraid that she would resent me for leaving her. Four very long years passed, and life in Canada kept us busy. But I hung onto the hope and dream that one day, I would be reunited with my daughter and my whole family would finally be together.

How did you feel when you were finally reunited with her?

My heart was whole again, and I wept for joy. For four years, a part of me had been missing. Now I felt complete. It was the best feeling ever. I hugged Van, and I didn't want to ever let her go. My family was reunited.

What else would you like readers to know?

For parents, I hope they cherish every single day they have with their children. Hug them, kiss them, and tell them how much you love them.

I was faced with a very difficult decision. To this day, I still have regrets that I left my child behind. I hope you never have to make a decision like this.

Vanessa and Bà Ngoại in Canada, 1997

Vanessa (age 3) in 1980, shortly after her father and sister escaped Vietnam

Dad and Linh at a refugee camp in Malaysia, 1980

Linh, Tuan, Loan, and Lan in Toronto in 1981

Vanessa (age 5)

Vanessa (age 6). Vanessa's aunt posed her in various parks to send photos to her family in Canada

Vanessa (age 6)

Vanessa (age 7)

Vanessa (age 8)
shortly before leaving
Vietnam in 1985

Vanessa (age 8), Tuan, Mom, and Dad in Canada, 1985

Mom and Bà Ngoại at her first Christmas in Canada

Vanessa's mom and dad, 1985

Vanessa (age 8) with Tuan in 1986. First winter in Canada

Dad and Vanessa (age 9) in New York City

Vanessa (age 11, second from left) with her family on holiday

Vanessa and her family today